# FIVE-STAR Solos

## 11 Colorful Piano Solos with Optional Duet Accompaniments

## DENNIS ALEXANDER

Choosing just the right piece for each student is one of the most important attributes of a good teacher. I love it when I hear things like, "Mr. A., can I please play the piece that Brenda played on the last recital?" or, "Mr. A., the piece that John played is one of the coolest pieces I've ever heard! Do you think I could play it?"

The books in the *Five-Star Solos* series provide students and teachers with a wide variety of pieces at graded levels. An array of styles, colors, tempos, and moods are included in each book. Ballads, waltzes, Latin pieces, contemporary sounds, and "showstoppers" all combine to make teaching fun and exciting. At the same time, students will be rewarded with music that sets them apart from the crowd! Have fun exploring page after page of music that will have students smiling and parents glowing. I hope that you find many new "favorites" in this series, and I wish you continued success and joy in your musical journey!

*Dennis Alexander*

*Dedicated to Noreen Wensley, a wonderful teacher and friend in Saskatoon, Saskatchewan*

Alfred Music.
P.O. Box 10003
Van Nuys, CA 91410-0003
alfred.com

ISBN-10: 1-4706-2639-X
ISBN-13: 978-1-4706-2639-6
Cover Photos
Piano keys: © Shutterstock.com / nav • Gold star: © Shutterstock.com / Yulia Glam

# SMOOTH MOVER

Dennis Alexander

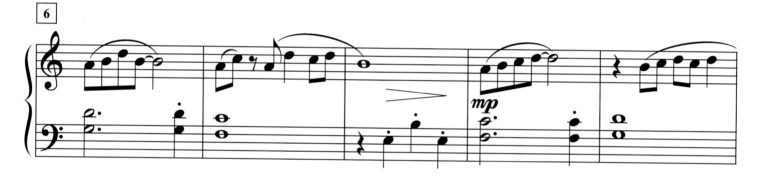

**Optional Duet Accompaniment:** Student plays one octave higher.

* When played as a duet, student does not pedal.

# MYSTICAL DANCE

Dennis Alexander

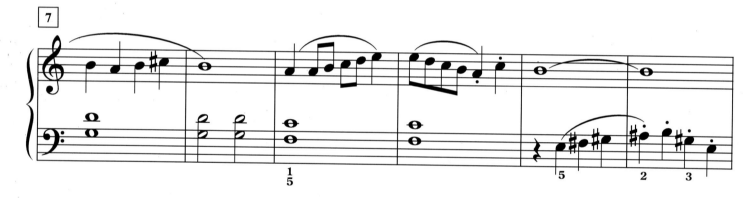

**Optional Duet Accompaniment:** Student plays one octave higher.

# Fearless Adventurer!

Dennis Alexander

**Optional Duet Accompaniment:** Student plays one octave higher.

# PIED PIPER'S MARCH

Dennis Alexander

**Optional Duet Accompaniment:** Student plays one octave higher.

*for Caitlin*

# THE LONELY FAWN

Dennis Alexander

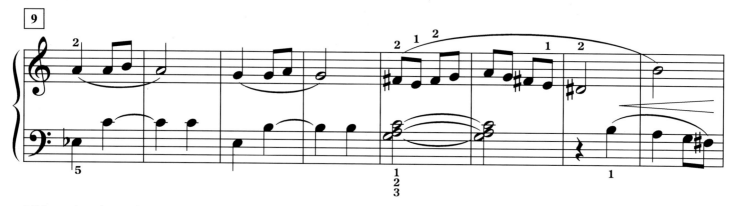

\* When played as a duet, student does not pedal.

**Optional Duet Accompaniment:** Student plays one octave higher.

# Boogie Gone Wild!

Dennis Alexander

**Optional Duet Accompaniment:** Student plays one octave higher.

# Thoughts of Yesterday

Dennis Alexander

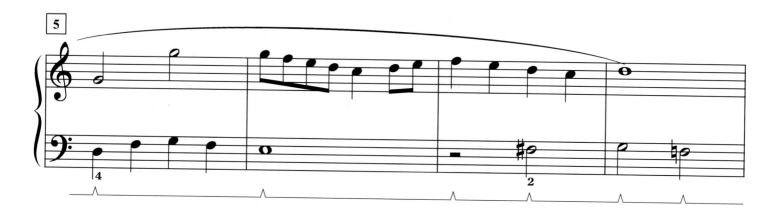

\* When played as a duet, student does not pedal.

**Optional Duet Accompaniment:** Student plays one octave higher.

**Optional Duet (cont.)**

# A BIT BEWILDERED!

Dennis Alexander

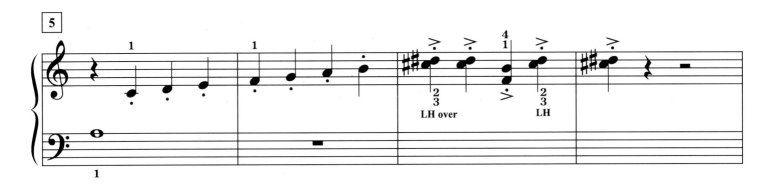

**Optional Duet Accompaniment:** Student plays one octave higher.

Optional Duet (cont.)

# Autumn Waltz

Dennis Alexander

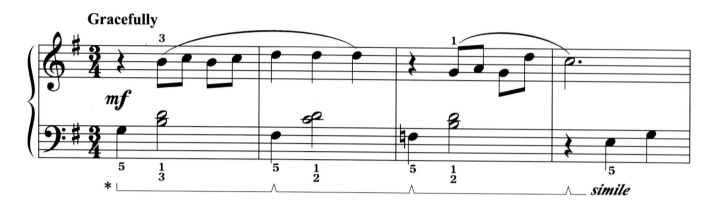

* When played as a duet, student does not pedal.

**Optional Duet Accompaniment:** Student plays one octave higher.

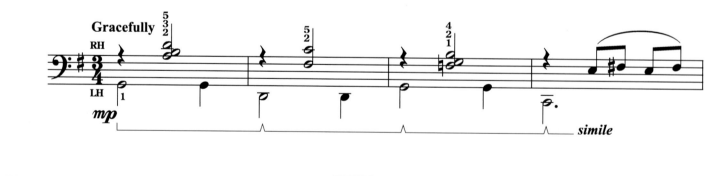

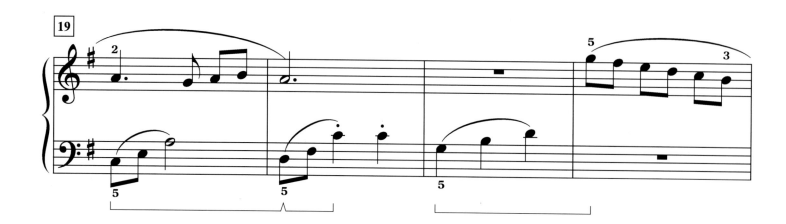

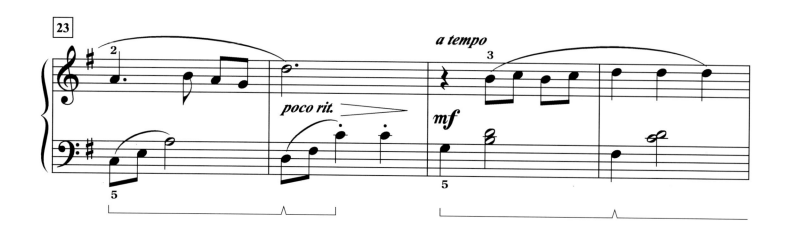

**Optional Duet (cont.)**

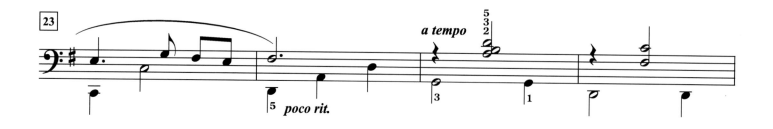

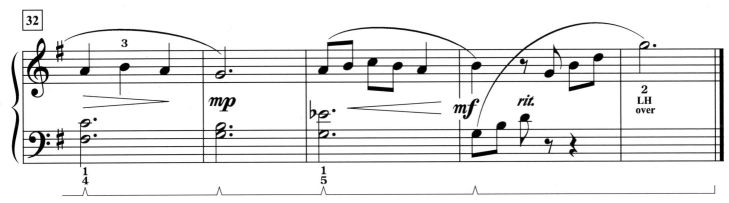

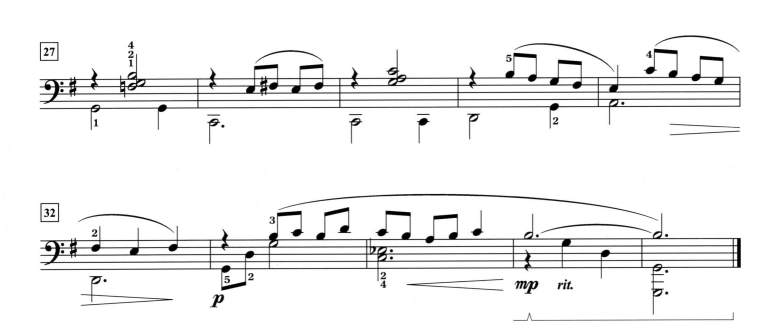

# Tahiti Tango

Dennis Alexander

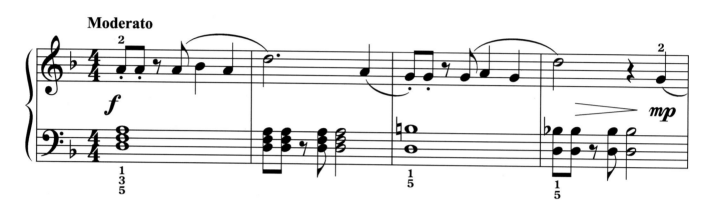

**Optional Duet Accompaniment:** Student plays one octave higher.

**Optional Duet (cont.)**

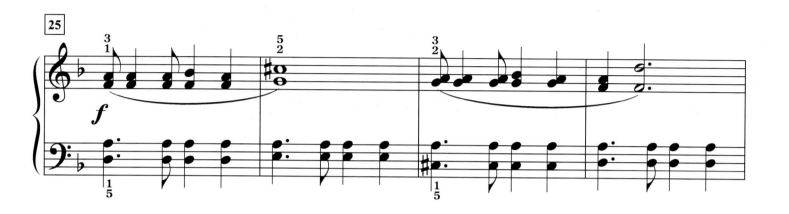

# JAMAICAN FESTIVAL

Dennis Alexander

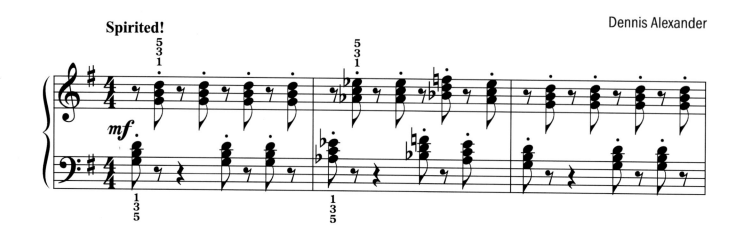

**Optional Duet Accompaniment:** Student plays one octave higher.

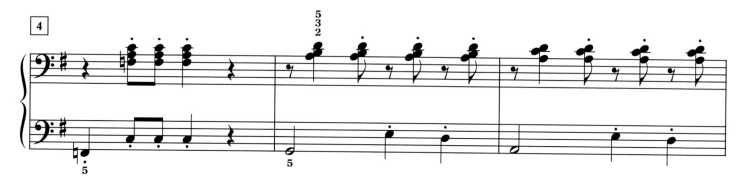

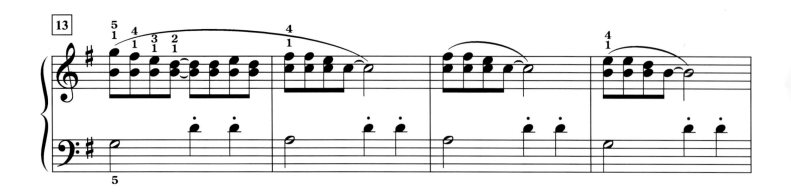

**Optional Duet (cont.)**

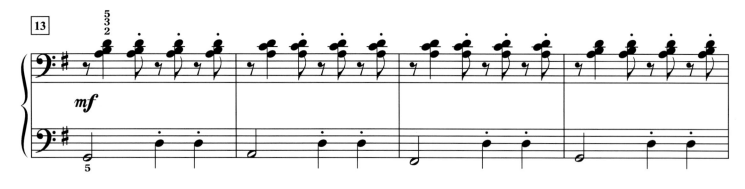

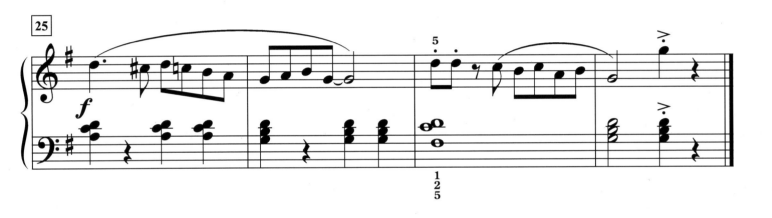